I HATE® FLORIDA

303 Reasons Why You Should, Too

D1558754

I HATE FLORIDA
303 Reasons Why You Should, Too

Paul Finebaum

CRANE HILL
PUBLISHERS

Birmingham, Alabama

Library of Congress Cataloging-in-Publication Data

Finebaum, Paul 1955-
    I hate Florida: 303 reasons why you should, too / by Paul Finebaum
      p.   cm.
    ISBN 1-57587-116-5
    1. University of Florida — Football — Miscellanea. 2. Florida Gators (Football team). — Miscellanea.
I. Title.
GV958.U523F55   1995
796.332'63'0975979–dc20   95-34957
                                                                   CIP

10   9   8   7   6   5   4   3   2   1

I HATE FLORIDA

I Hate Florida Because…

1. The movie *The Waterboy* was modeled after the boyhood of Steve Spurrier.

2. A hurricane recently hit Gainesville and did $2 million worth of improvements.

3. Terry Bowden's picture is on the wall of every post office in Gainesville.

4. The biggest difference between Steve Spurrier and puppies is that puppies usually stop whining when they grow up.

5. Tony George will be teaching a summer school class next year entitled "How to Lose the Big Game Before It Starts."

6. Florida has never won a national championship—oops—they won one by mistake!

7. Most schools like FSU have banners for their NCAA and ACC championships. Florida has them for the number of times it has been on NCAA probation.

8. The only reason Florida beat Auburn for the services of Emmitt Smith is because Pat Dye got to the youngster's home after the bidding closed.

9. Emmitt played for 3 different head coaches at Florida and hated every one of them.

10. The bumper sticker "Wait Until Next Year" has been the UF bookstore's No. 1 selling item for 105 consecutive years.

11. Gator fans think that "007" refers to the GPA of the Florida football team.

12. Give a Florida graduate a fish and he will eat for a day. Teach him to fish and he will sit in a boat and drink beer all day.

13. Gators are proof positive that you should never underestimate the power of stupid people in large groups.

14. The difference between a Gator cheerleader and an elephant is about twenty pounds.

15. If you want to make up the difference, force feed the elephant.

16. For his birthday, Steve Spurrier's wife, Jeri, bought him the hot-selling book *The Pocket Guide to Better Sex* and told him to start reading.

17. Mick Hubert's anthology of Florida football, *100 Years of NCAA Probation,* did not sell well last Christmas.

18. The book *I Hate FSU* did quite well, though.

19. If you want to keep a Gator out of your back yard, paint your yard like an endzone.

20. Jeri and Steve Spurrier have decided to take their vacation next spring on the Internet.

21. Lon Kruger checked into an Ocala mental hospital last winter complaining of "March Madness."

22. There are so many rough neighborhoods in Gainesville that the local motels ask customers to list next of kin on their registration.

23. Considering Florida's problems with the NCAA, the school has already put Colin Ferguson on retainer as a compliance officer.

24. Because football season is so busy in Gainesville, UF cheerleaders double up on Weight Watchers meetings in winter.

25. Spurrier once said, "Marriage is the only war in which you sleep with the enemy."

26. Spurrier also once said, "My wife always complained about not having outside interests, so I bought her a Weed Eater."

27. Spurrier is the only person known to man who can enter a room mouth first.

28. When Spurrier left Duke for Florida, the IQ of both places doubled.

29. Florida men are now refusing to marry kin unless they are at least third cousins.

30. Some Florida coeds are so ugly that local restaurants hand them doggie bags before they eat.

31. Florida Field now prohibits foreign cars from parking unless they can show a passport.

32. How do you find the Swamp? First you go east until you smell it, then you go south until you step in it.

33. The most popular song on frat row is "Purple Haze."

34. Florida fans refuse to drive through Auburn, Alabama, because they are afraid they'll get beaten.

35. Florida spelled backwards is ADIROLF.

36. You're right—it doesn't make any sense!

37. Terry Bowden is taking his family to Florida Field next summer because of the great memories of the stadium.

38. Bobby Bowden is going to do the same thing for his family.

39. There is still no one who knows how many Gators it takes to tackle a Nebraska Cornhusker.

40. Or how many it takes to tackle a Florida State Seminole.

41. Florida graduates get a free hunting license with their diploma.

42. The best thing to ever come out of Gainesville is I-75.

43. The only sign of intelligent life in Gainesville is the sign that reads "Tallahassee: 149 miles."

44. Vernon Maxwell majored in criminal justice while at UF and put his education to good use.

45. The best thing about living in Gainesville is that the average age is "deceased."

46. Emmitt Smith's fondest memory of Florida is having 3 different head coaches.

47. The only good thing about Gainesville is that it's only three hours away from Tallahassee.

48. Spurrier has such a large ego that he bows when it thunders.

49. Florida has a rehabilitation hospital for students who are Hooked on Phonics.

50. Gators believe that T.G.I.F. stands for "Toes Go in First."

51. Some Florida players think Dr. Pepper is the team physician.

52. Florida requires all entering freshmen to be able to spell SAT, ACT, and IQ.

53. The poll on which Florida has finished first most often is the FBI's Most Wanted.

54. Florida has a special course for teaching the vice presidents since Quayle.

55. Florida fraternities have a special contest in spring for the pledge with the worst case of athlete's foot.

56. The Florida business school has a course in how to read the Land's End catalog.

57. Gainesville has more Waffle House locations per square mile than any other college town in the SEC.

58. Gov. Jeb Bush likes the Gators because he can spell it.

59. To receive a degree from Florida, players must be able to write their name, age, and Social Security number without making more than 3 mistakes.

60. New Florida graduates are always upset because they have to learn to spell the name of another city.

61. If you ever doubted Steve Spurrier was a jerk, just ask Terry Dean.

62. All weddings on campus are toasted with a bottle of Gatorade.

63. Danny Wuerffel once said that he could have been a Rhodes Scholar except for his grades.

64. Errict Rhett thinks he was in *Gone with the Wind.*

65. Even a third-string freshman quarterback is enough to defeat Florida's defense.

66. Tony George thought he was related to George Foreman, but it turns out he has closer kinship to Boy George.

67. Chris Collingsworth teaches a class at UF called "How to Chase Women."

68. Kay Stephenson still believes that he was the first female quarterback in the SEC.

69. "Charmin" Harmon Wages once played for the Gators. What else needs to be said?

70. Galen Hall never met a chili dog he didn't like.

71. Florida players always enjoy spring break because they escape Mike Bianchi's column in the *Gainesville Sun.*

72. Norm Carlson was there when Ponce De Leon discovered Florida.

73. Steve Spurrier's wife buys the newspaper *Gator Bait* instead of Charmin for her guest bathrooms.

74. The new rule in Florida is plastic-only forks and knives at team meetings during bowl games.

75. Also, on future bowl trips, players must wear bulletproof vests and armor—but only at team meals.

76. G. E. Pyle, who coached at UF from 1909–1913, was really Gomer's father.

77. A seven-course meal in Gainesville is a six pack and a possum.

78. Spurrier ended his NFL career at Tampa Bay in 1976–so does most everyone else who plays there.

79. Ron Zook has a dartboard of Spurrier in his den and there's a poison dart through Spurrier's head.

80. Ben Hill Griffin Stadium at Florida Field is the stupidest sounding name in the SEC.

81. You have to hand it to the Florida staff for scheduling powerhouse opponents like Central Florida.

82. Apparently, Harvard and Yale were busy that day.

83. Florida president John Lombardi thinks he is related to Vince Lombardi.

84. UF athletic director Jeremy Foley has a sissy name.

85. Florida has the same colors as Auburn.

86. Jeremy Foley likes to brag that he is kin to Tom Foley, but not actually Tom Foley.

87. Spurrier once said, "I sure enjoyed winning the Heisman. But I am very thankful they didn't ask me to spell it."

88. Emmitt Smith once said, "Now, does going right mean I run away from my big toe or toward it?"

89. Florida's graduating class this year wants Carrot Top to speak at graduation.

90. Charles Barkley considered going to Florida until he found out the town only had 4 Pizza Huts.

91. It is now mandatory for Florida coeds to shave under their arms between April and June.

92. Florida fans order *Sports Illustrated* for the free phone instead of for the swimsuit issue.

93. UF fans believe the New York Stock Exchange is when a group of Northerners gets together to swap cows and pigs.

94. In honor of the city of Gainesville, UF fraternities serve their pledges Gainesburgers.

95. Only 19% of Florida fans own mouthwash.

96. And only 19% of them use it.

97. Some UF graduates thought the 1991 Gulf War was fought in Tampa Bay.

98. Steve Spurrier's idea of hell is the year FSU decides to join the SEC.

99. Spurrier's idea of hell Part 2 is if Terry ever replaces Bobby Bowden at Florida State.

100. Marilyn Manson was once a male cheerleader at Florida.

101. Jeremy Foley has a poster of Shelly Winters on his bedroom wall.

102. David Lamm once said on his radio show that safe sex can only be practiced on top of a bank safe.

103. John Reaves coined the saying "I was born at night, but it wasn't last night."

104. The University of Florida Gator has more teeth than the entire student body.

105. Emmitt Smith once said, "A mind is a terrible thing to waste. So I am donating mine to Florida."

106. People in Gainesville think a honeymoon is when lovers bare their buttocks toward a public building.

107. UF fans think the White House was named after Slappy White.

108. UF students can't understand why the show *Get Smart* is shown so often at freshmen orientation.

109. Gator players think the field is called "The Swamp" because that's what Terry Bowden always does to them in that stadium.

110. Florida fans were surprised to learn the movie *From Here to Eternity* was about Pearl Harbor and not about the NCAA's continuing visits to Gainesville.

111. *Playboy* featured an alligator in its series "Girls of the SEC" because it couldn't find a good-looking Florida coed.

112. If Microsoft was based in Gainesville we'd all be using The Winders operating system.

113. Florida fans still light candles every year on Lassie's birthday.

114. Emmitt Smith once said that racquetball was his favorite sport at UF. "I played for three hours and didn't lose a single ball," he explained.

115. Florida's home economics department has a course titled "Polish Gourmet Cooking."

116. Charley Pell once yelled at his team during halftime of the Miami game, "What's wrong with you guys? You're playing like a bunch of amateurs!"

117. Some Florida coeds think intercourse is the time off between classes.

118. Florida players know the 4 seasons well: football recruiting, losing to Tennessee, losing to Florida State, and the off-season.

119. Steve Spurrier's brain is always fresh—he's never used it.

120. Florida cheerleaders have sex only on days that have a "d" in them.

121. Spurrier has a new book coming out next fall called *The 100 Biggest Games I Choked In.*

122. Gators spelled backwards is SROTAG.

123. Sounds like a social disease, doesn't it?

124. Florida has toughened its entrance requirements; applicants are now required to type in their names.

125. The Gainesville airport would make a nice nuclear waste dump.

126. Before receiving their degree, Florida students must show proof of purchase for at least 2 textbooks.

127. Florida's liberal arts school requires a foreign language for in-state students—English.

128. Steve Spurrier's idea of Armageddon is being on a desert island with Terry and Bobby Bowden.

129. Spurrier said if that ever happened, suicide would be his only way out.

130. Steve Babik is a geek.

131. Spurrier once said, "I gave the sexual performance of my life last night. I'm just sorry my wife wasn't awake to see it."

132. To make a Gator laugh on Saturday, tell him a joke on Wednesday.

133. In Gainesville, the truck with the largest tires always has the right of way.

134. Fidel Castro had Florida to win in the Florida/Florida State game.

135. However, he bet on the wrong player in the knife fight prior to the game.

136. Most Gator law school graduates still think "Roe v. Wade" is a decision to be made before crossing a creek.

137. David Lamm's television show in Jacksonville is called *Lamm At Large* not *Lamm Is Large,* although both would be appropriate.

138. Lamm once told a date, "Love at first sight saves a lot of time."

139. Lamm also said, "If you think looks improve with the years, try attending a class reunion."

140. Steve Spurrier often contradicts himself—and he is usually right.

141. Florida fans are sick of hearing Mick Hubert scream, "Oh my!" after FSU touchdowns.

142. The tour guide for the city of Gainesville has a lonelier job than the Maytag repairman.

143. Shane Matthews actually believed the movie "Shane" was based on his life.

144. Jack Jackson tells people that he is Bo's brother.

145. But he won't tell anyone he is friends with Michael Jackson.

146. Brad Culpepper thinks that he is related to Dr Pepper.

147. Kerwin Bell believes that his grandmother was Tinker Bell.

148. And his grandfather was Taco Bell.

149. And his great-grandfather was Alexander Graham Bell.

150. His son will probably be named Dumb Bell.

151. Mike Bianchi, formerly of the *Gainesville Sun*, has a Spurrier dartboard in his bathroom.

152. Larry Kennedy used to brag that his uncle was Teddy.

153. UF ranks fourth among all U.S. schools in patents issued.

154. One of those patents is for the inflatable dartboard, another is for the waterproof towel.

155. A couple of years ago Florida fans showed their class by spitting on the wife of the Tennessee coach.

156. Last year, some eager Florida senior enlisted early for NFL draft day.

157. UF offers a freshman class in remedial sex.

158. David Lamm willed his head to science. They are going to use it for an experimental rock garden.

159. Steve Spurrier once said he wouldn't hurt a flea.

160. Of course the reason is he has so many of them.

161. Mike Bianchi is fond of saying, "I have no prejudices. I hate everybody equally."

162. In Gainesville a byte is what your pit bull "Hoss" done to cousin Jethro.

163. And cache is what you need when you run out of food stamps.

164. Lon Kruger can't get arrested in Gainesville during football season.

165. Norm Carlson once owned Mr. Ed.

166. The Stephen C. O'Connell Center is the ugliest building in Florida.

167. University of Florida computer science majors think a web site is usually in the attic.

168. Gators are proof of reincarnation, because you can't get that dumb in just one lifetime.

169. Bull Gators–the name says it all.

170. Dr. John Lombardi buys his glasses at Kmart.

171. Gator basketball head coach Billy Donovan has a hard time teaching players that dribbling is not the same thing as drooling.

172. The prettiest view of Gainesville is through a rearview mirror.

173. David Lamm once said, "The best thing about football is it only takes four quarters to finish a fifth."

174. Gainesville is such a hick town that the town hooker has to stand under a flashlight.

175. Some of the UF cheerleaders are so ugly they buy their makeup from Barnum and Bailey.

176. A diploma from UF is about as valuable as David Lamm's autograph.

177. Jeremy Foley was so ugly at birth that his mother was arrested for littering.

178. Foley was so ugly at birth that his doctor slapped his mother.

179. Foley was so ugly at birth that his mother breast-fed him with a straw.

180. Steve Spurrier grows taller when he takes Viagra.

181. UF likes to brag that more than 80% of its players are from Florida. The rest of the country is too smart to want to go there.

182. Emmitt Smith once said that his fondest memory of Florida was leaving it.

183. And he says he still can't get the smell out of his clothes.

184. Steve Spurrier has vowed to work on the UF defense next season. He has even learned how to spell it.

185. Gainesville claims to be the home of the "World's largest sewage flume."

186. Gregg Allman is a big Gator fan.

187. UF players are tested for distemper twice a month.

188. Once Elvis was kicked out of Florida practice for trying to eat the Gator.

189. John Lombardi has a picture of Marla Maples in his private study.

190. Norm Carlson has a picture of Aunt Bee in his house.

191. Steve Spurrier has a picture of Goober in his office.

192. Sans-A-Belt sells more slacks than Levis does in Gainesville.

193. Steve Spurrier thinks that the movie *It's a Wonderful Life* is about him.

194. Florida cheerleaders don't like to lie out in the summer because the heat might melt their plastic surgery.

195. David Lamm has a secret crush on Betty Crocker.

196. Only at a school like Florida could a player like Emmitt Smith finish less than seventh in the Heisman Trophy balloting.

197. O. J. Simpson is a closet UF fan because he enjoys people who are always trying to run away from authorities.

198. Simpson considered Florida over USC until he heard they were already over the salary cap.

199. Former UF running back Neal Anderson used to tell dates that he was the first man to walk on the moon.

200. James Jones, the former All–SEC rusher, used to tell dates that he was the famous actor.

201. You know a Gator is about to say something smart when he starts his sentence with "A FSU Seminole once told me ..."

202. Most UF football players believe most sentences end in an appeal.

203. If you breed a Florida Gator with a groundhog you're guaranteed six more weeks of bad football.

204. Norman Sloan left Florida complaining of illness and fatigue—the fans were sick and tired of him.

205. John Lombardi once said, "We don't need to replace our coaches. Instead, we need to find a way to get rid of the alumni."

206. Most Florida players' lists of accomplishments read like rap sheets.

207. Spurrier got his team in the right frame of mind at the 1998 UF/FSU game by saying, "Don't worry. If we lose we can always blame the coaching."

208. The bestselling placard every year at the end of the Florida–FSU game is "Wait until next year."

209. Will Rogers obviously never met Steve Spurrier.

210. Jeri Spurrier once said, "People ask me to speak about sex and marriage, but being Steve's wife, I don't know anything about them."

211. Spurrier chose to attend Florida over Tennessee because it was easier to spell.

212. David Lamm once said, "Some people hate Steve Spurrier like poison. I just hate him regular."

213. Spurrier wears a visor during games so that no one can see his brain sleep.

214. Jeb Bush has a secret fantasy about sleeping with an alligator.

215. Florida fans think that catfish has to be fried 9 times to get all of its lives.

216. Some fans think that a racist is a person who drives on the NASCAR circuit.

217. Followers of the UF program think that *America's Most Wanted* is about their football team.

218. The Florida journalism school requires every graduate to subscribe to *The Weekly Reader.*

219. Florida business school students believe that Dow Jones is Ed "Too Tall" Jones's brother.

220. The athletic training special on Friday night at Yon Hall Dorm is Broken Leg of Lamb.

221. The Florida cheerleaders have a Fax-on-Demand service on Tuesdays and a Sex-on-Demand service on Fridays.

222. The captain of the cheerleading squad is the girl with the smallest fever blister.

223. The Swamp spelled backward is Pmaws, which sounds likes something you might take Midol for.

224. Instead of using a driver's license, a UF graduate may now show his belt buckle for admission into Florida Field.

225. Ben Hill Griffin used to tell people that Andy Griffith was his father.

226. Most Gators find that being a freshman can be the six hardest years of their lives.

227. They also believe that Gatorade is a UF assistant coach.

228. Some Florida fans still light candles on Winnie the Pooh's birthday.

229. The town of Gainesville has a smell similar to cow manure.

230. Jeremy Foley almost didn't get the job because he misspelled Gators on the application form.

231. He spelled the nickname "Gaters" because of all the tailgate parties.

232. David Lamm is a born-again cretin.

233. John Lombardi thinks cellular phones are normal phones with cellophane wrapped around them.

234. Mick Hubert's neck is so dirty that he has swamp around the collar.

235. Before he came to UF, Norm Carlson handled public relations for Lewis and Clark's expedition.

236. Carlson quit gambling after the Civil War–he had the South plus the points.

237. Spurrier has instituted a "Don't ask, don't tell" policy among UF recruits.

238. Spurrier constantly calls NFL clubs suggesting they hire Bobby Bowden.

239. Norm Carlson looks so old that it seems like he gave the pallbearers the slip.

240. Gainesville is such a conservative town that it once banned Flash Gordon because the mayor didn't like what he was flashing.

241. The food served at UF campus restaurants is so bad that the only card they take is Blue Cross.

242. Steve Spurrier once said, "Suicide is the last thing a person should do."

243. David Lamm comes from a sex-crazed family. His grandfather died at age 104–he was shot by a jealous husband.

244. The captain of the UF cheerleading squad made the band in high school.

245. She also made the football team and the basketball team.

246. Billy Donovan is still trying to teach his players that a foul ball has nothing to do with its smell.

247. Success hasn't gone to Steve Spurrier's head—just to his mouth.

248. The Florida athletic department now has a course on how to fight before a game and not get caught.

249. Without Danny Wuerrfel it will likely be another 105 years before Florida gets another national football championship.

250. Some Florida coeds are so fat that they have unlisted dress sizes.

251. David Lamm was so ugly as a youngster that his father went around showing people the baby picture that came with the wallet.

252. Steve Spurrier's autobiography sold like wildfire. It was so bad that everyone burned it.

253. Flying out of Gainesville is so dangerous that the longest line in the airport is at the flight insurance counter.

254. The only thing Florida and Florida State students have in common is that both were accepted to Florida.

255. The campus bar recently hired a midget bartender to make the drinks look bigger.

256. Steve Spurrier is so cheap that he had Baggies sewn into his pockets so he could take soup home from the restaurant.

257. Spurrier has not smiled since the day his doctor told him he can have only 1 mouth.

258. David Lamm once said to a friend, "My wife is something. She has cut back on sex to twice a week." His friend said, "Don't feel bad. I know a guy she cut out completely."

259. UF graduates hang their diplomas in the rear windows of their cars so they can park in "handicapped" spaces.

260. If you drive slowly enough through Gainesville they are likely to give you a diploma.

261. Mike Bianchi was once dropped as a member of the human race.

262. Spurrier said he hates sex in the movies. He tried it once and the seat folded on him.

263. Jeremy Foley goes to the dentist as often as Bugs Bunny does.

264. John Lombardi tries to dress just like Ward Cleaver.

265. When addressing FSU graduates, most University of Florida graduates say "Would you like fries with that, sir?"

278. Florida players quit bleeding in the fourth quarter of the Sugar Bowl loss to FSU—they ran out of blood.

279. Spurrier is so conceited that his head has its own zip code.

280. Larry Guest recently finished his last book—at least people hope it's his last book.

281. Terry Dean didn't play much as quarterback for Florida his senior year. But at least his dry-cleaning bill for his uniform was down.

282. Spurrier often tells his players, "People who live in glass houses don't have much of a sex life."

283. The UF football team is considering changing its name to the "Opossums" because they play dead at home and get killed on the road.

284. After losing again to FSU, Jeremy Foley said, "If lessons are learned in defeat, our team is really getting a great education."

285. Spurrier is in a class by himself—or rather a lack of class all by himself.

286. Florida prohibits roller skating on campus but allows football boosters to buy players new cars.

287. When Charley Pell arrived at Florida he said, "I don't expect to win enough games to be put on NCAA probation. I just want to win enough to warrant an investigation."

288. Charley Pell might have been a better prophet than football coach.

289. The only time Steve Spurrier didn't run up the score was when he took the SAT.

290. Steve Spurrier is as graceless in defeat as he is in victory.

291. Spurrier has obviously never heard the expression "Pride is hard to swallow, but it will go down."

292. The Gators used to have ice on their sidelines until the guy with the recipe graduated.

293. Danny Wuerrfel once said, "I could have been a Rhodes Scholar except my name wasn't Rhodes."

294. David Lamm is fond of saying, "The best way to avoid infections from insect bites is to quit biting insects."

295. The hardest math class most Florida football players take is "Subtraction: Addition's Tricky Friend."

296. John Lombardi is a perfectionist. If he were married to Sharon Stone, he would expect her to cook.

297. Emmitt Smith found a lot of holes while rushing for the Gators. The only thing he couldn't seem to find was the library.

298. When it was suggested to Steve Spurrier that the school burn Bobby Bowden in effigy, Spurrier said, "Heck, let's go ahead and burn him in Gainesville."

299. When Spurrier heard they were giving out brains, he was in another line waiting for a second helping of mouth.

300. They gave Spurrier an unlimited budget when he arrived at UF, and he exceeded it.

301. Spurrier believes in the 2–party rule for his players: Party all day.

302. Party all night.

303. The biggest difference between God and Steve Spurrier is that God doesn't believe that he is Steve Spurrier.